letters from
LOVE

by

flavia zenari

Copyright

IBSN: 978-0-646-83983-7
Title: Letters from Love
Author: Flavia Zenari
© 2021, Flavia Zenari
flavia.zenari@gmail.com
flaviazenari.com

Cover Art by Justine Espinueva
Internal Illustrations by Edoardo Lo Vecchio

ALL RIGHTS RESERVED. This book contains material protected under International and Federal Copyright Laws and Treaties.

Any unauthorised reprint or use of this material is prohibited. No part of this book may be reproduced or transmitted in any form or by any means, electronic or mechanical, including photocopying, recording or otherwise, without the prior written permission of the author.

*A dedication to all I have, do, and will come to love.
For all the support, patience, wisdom, and unconditional love
that has been a catalyst for this book.
The gratitude I have for each one of you is infinite.*

What a beautiful unfolding is this journey of life.

– Flavia Zenari

In times of darkness, remember that you are the light

Breath Is Life

Make a practice of welcoming love
into every cell of your body –
befriend your breath as though it is
your dearest friend –
as you inhale,
breathe in the energy of life,
and feel it radiate throughout your entire being.

Here To Stay

For those lonely days
when you feel as though the world is bleak and empty,
take comfort in knowing love is here in every sound,
in every sight
whether it be the brightest day,
or the darkest of nights –
love is here to stay,
always.

Just as You Are

The dimples in your skin,
the creases of your eyes,
the slight dip below your mouth,
a roadmap to love,
absolute perfection –
just as you are.

Faith

The distance between what you seek
and what you perceive as reality –
whenever faith is lost in love
it hides away in corners out of sight,
whenever found in love
it reveals itself smiling ear to ear comforted in your trust –
always keep faith
in love.

Clear Sight

If I could give you any gift in the world,
I would give you the gift of seeing yourself
through love's eyes.

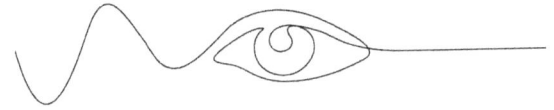

Rising in Love

You know of the expression, 'falling in love',
but have you ever tried perhaps,
rising with it instead?

Treasure Hunt

As you journey your way through life
you will encounter rocky paths,
river crossings,
and unpaved roads;
in each of these passageways sits hidden treasures
awaiting your discovery.

Foundations of Love

Love exists as the foundation of who you are –
think of love as the clay from which you were moulded,
as the pillars that give you strength to withstand
all that moves by you –
love is who you are when all layers are stripped bare.

Master the Mind

Your mind is a sponge
that feeds off sensory experiences;
sights,
sounds,
touch,
smell –
surround yourself with experiences
that will help your mind grow into a compassionate,
encouraging
tool.

Creativity

Your heart
is the birthplace
of creativity.

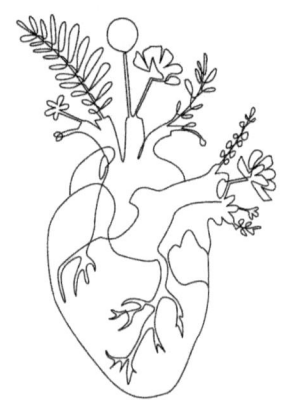

11:11

11:11 —
that's a sign that love is around.

Soul Rider

When your eyes lock,
your mouth curves,
and your heart pounds skipping a beat,
when nothing else in this universe matters
and all matter dissipates into nothingness –
that is love
sending waves through your soul.

Fear Less

Whole-heartedly in love's presence,
fear cannot exist.

Look and You Shall Find

Within the simple pleasures of life, you can find love,
in a sunset,
a cool breeze on a summer's day,
or in the smile of a stranger –
love is all around.

Cycles of Bloom

A flower does not mourn the loss of its beauty
when its petals fall –
so do not mourn the changes of your vessel,
as love sees
that as the seasons change
richer and more vibrant flowers
are to bloom.

A Tender Reminder

Have you ever noticed
that the word heart
contains the word 'hear' –
just a tender reminder
to always listen to
what your heart has to say.

Your Greatest Ally

There are times where you may doubt yourself –
your choices,
your appearance,
your feelings –
in these moments of doubt
question yourself,
are these thoughts kind?
Are they true?
And are they words love would speak?

Wisdom Within

Love is a wise teacher –
within the centre of love
you will uncover great wisdom.

Lightly

Let there be an air of lightness in all you do –
lightly step into your mornings
as gentle as a wave ripples its way through a picturesque lake –
let lightness be the lantern that guides you on your way,
and the hand that draws you closer to your heart.

Comfort Zone

Outside the realm of comfort
exists an unknown space
which often the mind fears –
but fear not,
for love knows that outside this realm of comfort
is growth,
and growth sustains life itself.

Heart Full

What makes your heart full?
What fills your heart with joy and wonder?
Whatever it may be,
fill your life up with as much of these things
that you possibly can.

Your Birthright

Whenever you may believe you are not deserving of love
remember your birthright is,
and always will be,
love.

Peace on Earth

If it is peace on earth that you seek
free from war and unnecessary suffering,
you must first begin by harmonising the internal –
harmony and unity begin within.

We Are Connected

So much of the suffering felt in this world
is from the belief
that we are completely separate from others –
love will always show you
just how connected we are.

Watered with Kindness

Surround yourself with those that lift you up
not those that bring you down –
as a plant grows when it is watered,
so too can you grow when watered
with kindness
by those around you.

A Dance of Love

This life
is not a race
to reach a final destination –
be that a graduation,
a job,
a marriage,
or a child –
this life is a dance of moments –
the journey itself is the experience of love.

Punctually Present

In the curves of the letters,
in the spaces between words,
in each punctuation
love's echoing voice can be heard.

Gently

It is okay to be gentle with yourself,
to be gentle with who you are becoming,
one does not rush a baby to walk,
nor do you need to rush your progress –
softly
slowly
with love's guidance
you will arrive exactly
when you need to.

Be Free

Learn to bring back
the playfulness
of childhood –
grant your creativity the freedom to run wild,
jump in puddles,
skip down the street,
roll down grassy hills –
the child within you is waiting to be free again.

Rise Again

Yesterday's happenings
do not define today's happiness –
just as the sun rises each morning
you can choose to rise again each day.

From Fear to Love

The greatest journey
you will embark on
is the journey from fear,
to love.

Nature's Teachings

Look at the relationship between the fish
and the river –
the fish flow amongst the presence of the water
in perfect unison,
uniting with the current,
becoming one with their surroundings –
take note of what nature can teach you,
all the answers you need are right here.

Safety Net

Go out into the world with fearlessness,
love will be your safety net
your life raft –
with this fearlessness
your life begins anew.

Spread Your Love

Remember –
love did not create the rules you have surrounding it,
it does not judge you for how you express,
or show it;
you are free to spread and share love
through whatever small ways you can.

Mirrored

Feel safety in love's arms,
warmth in its touch,
presence in its smile,
and the universe in its eyes –
see,
love is just like you.

Seek Inward

You do not need to seek outwardly for love
for it has
and always will be
within you.

Let Love Guide

The truest sense of freedom
comes from the shedding of the conditioning
you have been taught to believe –
let go,
and let love guide.

Home at Heart

Home can be a place
but it can also be a feeling;
home can be found within the doorframe of your heart –
you are at home
when you are within.

Courage

Let courage be the catalyst
to transform your fear
into love.

Awaken to Love

Love has the power to move mountains,
to shift shorelines,
to shake the ground beneath which you stand –
love has the power to awaken the truth
within us all.

To Feel

When you try to understand love intellectually
you miss the essence of what it is –
when you attempt to define it
you cage something which cannot be confined –
when you judge it
you forget the reason for its existence –
try instead,
to just feel it.

Laughter Is the Greatest Nourishment

Laugh!
For every time you laugh love grows
and grows,
it expands with each belly roar,
with each giggle,
with every cackle and with each bellow –
laughter feeds love as it feeds you.

Let Your Heart Break Open

When your heart breaks,
allow it to break open –
allow love to find its way into each crevice,
filling the spaces with its wholeness.

It's Never Too Late

It often takes the nearing of an end to one's life
to recognise the importance of matters
true to the heart –
but it does not need to take an ending for this realisation,
you have the choice to recognise it,
now.

One and All

In the starry night sky,
in the darkness up so high
in the depths of the earth
below your feet you were birthed,
of the land and of the sea
from a life-giving tree –
you are earth,
you are me,
you are everything
you see.

What Is Love?

Are you blinded by love?
Does it cloud your vision in a foggy haze?
Does it shield you from truths?

Or is it truth that it reveals?
Is it clarity that it brings?
And is it sight that it restores?

Your Never-Ending Supply

Imagine now
in this moment,
all of the people on this earth
embracing one another with love –
take a moment to feel that energy
and know that energy resides within you
at all times,
whenever you may need it.

Reconnect

That which seeks to separate,
seeks to disconnect us from love –
that which seeks to unite us,
seeks to connect us back to love.

The Power of Speech

The spoken word has within it a great power –
In each word you grace upon others in the day
let them be softly spoken whispers
of beauty
whose messages reach far
and wide.

You Are Ready

As the caterpillar enters the cocoon and emerges as a butterfly,
you too can enter love's cocooned sanctuary,
ready for your own transformation.

Remember

Beyond the body,
the physical
beyond the mind and matter,
there is a deeper knowing of your true nature –
love is here to remind you
of what you may have forgotten –
that you are the divine
in movement.

The Heart Knows

The heart knows a depth of truth –
trust this knowing.

In Plain Sight

A warm cup of tea on a cold stormy night,
a helping hand during times of fright,
the compassion of a friend guiding you toward the light,
these are love's appearances
in everyday sight.

Precious Cargo

Take all the time you need to heal;
you are as precious as the rarest gem found here on earth –
let yourself shine again.

Be Here Now

Be still –
just for a minute
be here
now,
with love.

Uniquely Yours

Your uniqueness is your gift –
do not worry of your differences,
but embrace them as your distinctive offerings to the world.

Love's Voices

A sound as sweet as the bird's songs at sunrise,
as blissful as the wind waving its way through the trees,
as angelic as the strumming of the harpsicord –
let love fill your ears with the soft sounds of its voice,
the sound to which all life breathes.

Your True Nature

You are so supported,
so loved,
so divine –
recall your true nature,
your nature of pure love.

One Small Step

Ask yourself right now,
how can I bring more love into my day?
Just one choice in the direction of love can have a profound effect.

The Wind's Messenger

Allow your love to flow through the earth's atmosphere,
carried through the wings of the wind,
finding its way
to all those in need.

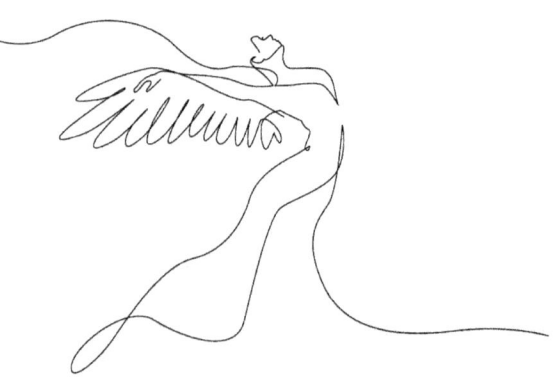

Life-Giving Sun

Golden rays of sunlight shine upon the earth
giving it energy
and sustaining life –
let the sun be a model of the nourishment that can be offered
when you shine light upon others.

Vow to You

If you are able to dedicate your life to love
I promise that it will forever be present,
aware,
consistent –
there is no greater power that can break the bond that you and love have.

Present

You may not feel love some days,
nor may you see it,
but it is here in her eyes,
in his smile,
in their laughter,
in your heart.

The Body Speaks

If each cell of your body had a voice,
what would it say?
Each ache,
pain,
problem or pestering,
has within it a message –
the body speaks,
it is time to listen.

Threaded Through

From heart to heart,
soul to soul,
mind to mind,
a web is weaved throughout space and time –
we are all intricately threaded together in a web so complex and divine.

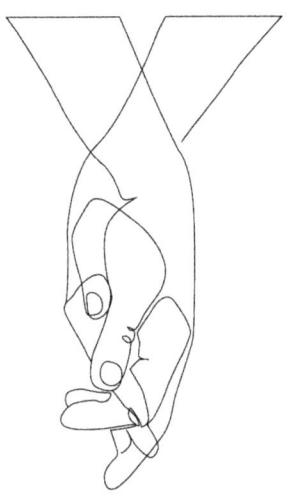

Child-Like Wonder

Journey into the unknown
with the same excitement
as a child who ventures
into their imagination –
curious,
carefree,
courageous.

Creation

When you engage in acts of creation
you are connected to the energy of love –
creativity is a direct line to love.

Abundantly

Fill up your cup from love's fountain,
fill yourself up
beyond the brim,
so that you overflow to those around you –
here you have an unlimited supply.

Always Loved

Love does not separate,
judge or divide –
love embraces,
unites and accepts.

Eternally

Time as it stands in its minutes,
hours,
days,
months,
and years,
begins to age all matter and life –
love is amongst the lucky few that time does not age,
nor diminish –
it is eternal.

A Miracle of Life

You being born is a miracle,
the fact of your existence is proof
that you are a miracle
of life.

Glimpses of Perfection

That momentary awareness of contentment,
bliss,
you have been there,
even if it was just for a moment –
the glimpse of pure perfection that exists in the universe,
this is being present with love.

Love Hurts? Love Heals

Some people may believe that 'love hurts' through heartbreak,
betrayal,
and other sorrows –
this, however,
is not an expression of love,
but of the hurt experienced by the touching of emotional wounds –
it is not in love's power to hurt you,
but it is through its power that you can heal.

Dream Big

Do not allow others to dampen your dreams,
conjure up the greatest life you can imagine
and know wholeheartedly
that your dreams are being supported by love,
at all times.

Daily Rituals

Mealtimes exist to remind you to nourish yourself with food,
and love is just as necessary to life,
as is food –
make note of creating space,
and time,
to bring love into your life throughout your day.

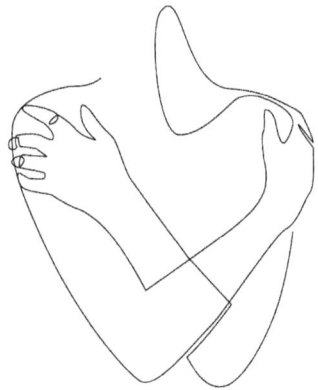

Navigation

Let your heart be the compass
to guide you
to your next step.

Your Task

I task you with the mission of finding a diamond,
not one that can be found in a mine
or in a jeweller's store,
but one that can be found
within you.

You and Love Are One

Let these words
be a marking
of all that you are
in your core –
let them be a stamp on your heart,
reminding you that you
and love
share far more than you realise.

Two Phrases

Thank you,

I love you –

two simple phrases with the power to change another's life.

La Luna

The moon teaches us
that within the darkness,
that is when our brightest light
can be seen.

Love's Equation

To the lovers,
the lovely,
the loved and those learning,
there is no one left out of love's equation,
even those that do not feel love's embrace –
know that it exists in multiplication through you.

May All Your Wishes Come True

When you wish upon a star which shoots across the sky,
or blow a breath upon a candle
squeezing your eyes tight –
know that love is always listening
and planning its arrival.

Symphony of Love

Sing that tune
that melody
that is so familiar to love's ears –
the song of celebration chorused throughout your life,
that is the sound that gives love life.

Infinite

All encompassing,
all engulfing,
omniscient and omnipresent,
there is nowhere love cannot reach,
see,
touch,
hear,
or feel.

Moth to a Flame

That space in your chest
with its fire burning a red so crimson and bright
acts like a beacon in the night –
love's energy guides even the darkest to the light.

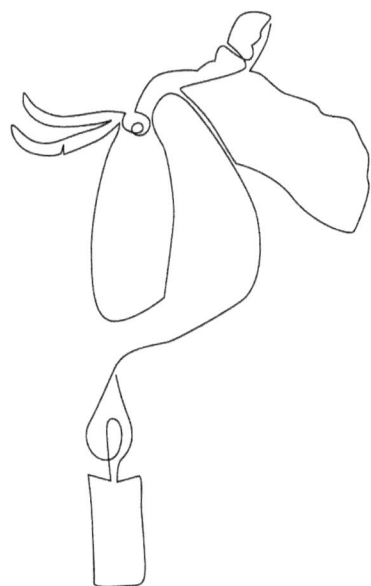

Let Go

You are an expression of the highest form of love,
so pure,
so deep –
allow yourself
to drop away
anything that makes you believe
otherwise.

Measures of Wealth

There is a tendency to admire those with luxuries
and monetary wealth,
yet people fail to see the wealth in those
with a full heart
and a clear mind –
wealth can be measured in more ways than one.

Departed but Never Forgotten

Even though they may be gone,
there is a presence of love that threads its way from them
and into you –
you will feel it as a gentle tapping on your heart's door.

Boundless

Have you ever noticed
that although you may be halfway across the world
with seas separating land
and lengths too far for legs to take,
love still finds its way to you –
it will never be bound
by space
or physical limitations.

Love the Skin You Are In

Your body is your temple,
your sacred vessel
transporting you through this life,
make sure to tend to yourself as you would tend to a beautiful garden –
love the skin you are in.

Manifestation

The universe is so vast,
expansive,
and limitless,
a place full of infinite possibilities –
you are the master of love's creation.

The Ride of Your Life

Wide awake,
sleepless nights,
tossing turning,
stomach full of butterflies,
beaming smiles,
glistening eyes,
one epic rollercoaster ride.

Unexpected Arrival

You will find love appearing
at the most unexpected of times,
a spontaneity in its existence –
be ready
for a welcomed surprise.

Follow Your Intuition

Your intuition is your inner guidance,
when you are confused by the voices of the mind
sink into your intuitive knowing,
and follow the highest calling of love.

Float Freely

See how gently a feather floats upon the breeze;
effortlessly flowing
with the natural movement of the wind –
in times of uncertainty,
remember the feather
and embody its teachings,
flowing softly
and gently
with ease,
amongst the winds of life.

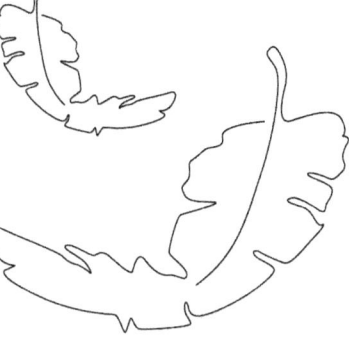

An Open Heart

To reach a state of compassion
and kindness for all
is the purest expression of love –
open your heart that little bit more
and you will feel.

Love's Packages

Love comes in all shapes and sizes,
a purple rectangle for you,
and a blue circle for your friend,
perhaps an orange hexagon for your neighbour!
No matter the visual or texture
in spirit,
love never truly changes.

A Well of Warmth

I wish you knew just how much love is present
in your life,
you are a part of love
as love is a part of you –
you are woven together like a wicker well,
catching everything which makes you feel warmth.

Worthy

The simple fact that you exist,
makes you worthy
of love.

True Love

Life is not meant to be easy all of the time –
life is not made to be without hills,
bumps
and rock-strewn edges,
life is not meant to be without triggers,
and insecurities –
but if amidst this you can find true connection,
and open communication,
you can find an anchor during the passing of the tides,
a raft to aid you through the unsettling seas,
and arms to embrace you through your past and your fears –
you can find,
true love.

Love Is

For love is
the essence
of the universe.

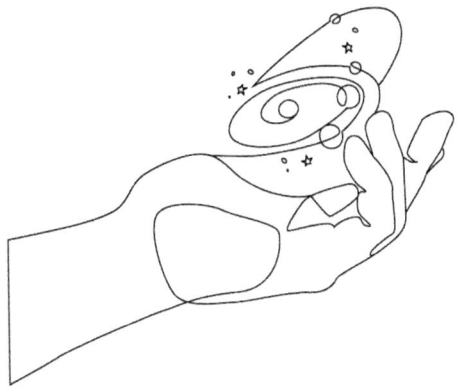

Empty your mind, connect to your heart, and write....

About the Author

Flavia Zenari is an Australian based poet and writer with a Bachelor of Arts in Anthropology and a Master of Social Change and Development.

Her passion in life is to cultivate a remembrance of our divine nature through conscious living. To her, living consciously means to live with awareness of our thoughts, energies, emotions, and actions, being acutely aware of our place in not only our inner and immediate world, but society and the universe at large. By opening the eyes, ears, hearts, and minds of readers she hopes to foster this sense of self-awareness.

Her writing includes both poetry as well as reflective, self-development pieces, assisting individuals to reconnect back to their true nature.

Having had lived experience of mental health challenges, and having also worked in the mental health field, she hopes to inspire and assist others in their life journey, guiding them through their own discovery of self-awareness, growth, and inner peace.

www.ingramcontent.com/pod-product-compliance
Lightning Source LLC
Chambersburg PA
CBHW070847160426
43192CB00012B/2343